COULD A WALRUS PLAY THE SAXOPHONE?

And Other Questions About Animals

Paul Mason

Raintree is an imprint of Capstone Global Library
Limited, a company incorporated in England and
Wales having its registered office at 7 Pilgrim Street,
London, EC4V 6LB – Registered company number:
6695582

To contact Raintree:
Phone: 0845 6044371
Fax: + 44 (0) 1865 312263
Email: myorders@raintreepublishers.co.uk.
Customers from outside the UK please telephone
+44 1865 312262.

Text © Capstone Global Library Limited 2014
First published in hardback in 2014
The moral rights of the proprietor have been asserted.

Edited by Dan Nunn, Rebecca Rissman,
    and John-Paul Wilkins
Designed by Steve Mead
Picture research by Mica Brancic
Production by Sophia Argyris
Originated by Capstone Global Library Ltd
Printed and bound in China by CTPS

ISBN 978 1 406 25946 9 (hardback)
17 16 15 14 13
10 9 8 7 6 5 4 3 2 1

British Library Cataloguing in Publication Data
Mason, Paul.
Could a walrus play the saxophone? and other
questions about animals. -- (Questions you never
thought you'd ask)
590.2-dc23
A full catalogue record for this book is available from
the British Library.

Acknowledgements
We would like to thank the following for permission
to reproduce photographs: Getty Images pp. 7
(Gallo Images/Federico Veronesi), 9 (Flickr/© 2006
Sean McCann), 23 (Peter Arnold/Jeffrey L. Rotman);
Science Photo Library p. 21 (Visuals Unlimited, Inc./
Eric Tourneret); Shutterstock pp. 4 orchestra (©
Ferenc Szelepcsenyi), 4 walrus (© ericlefrancais), 4
saxophone (© kuznetcov_konstantin), 5 walrus (© yui),
5 saxophone (© kuznetcov_konstantin), 6 (© jorisvo),
8 earwig (© Scott Hussey), 8 lady's ear (© Tatjana
Romanova), 10 man in swimming gear (© Lilyana
Vynogradova), 10 water background (© Clover), 10
medusa (© Jiri Vaclavek), 11 man in swimming gear (©
Lilyana Vynogradova), 11 toilet (© Jiri Hera), 11 plastic
bucket (© Andrey Eremin), 12 cow (© Dudarev Mikhail),
12 bomb explosion (© James Thew), 13 (© majeczka),
14 (© wtamas), 15 earthworm (© D. Kucharski & K.
Kucharska), 15 soil background (© PhotoHouse), 16
detective with magnifying glass (© Richard Peterson),
16 green plastic plate with crumbs (© Jaimie Duplass),
16 bloodhound dog (© Susan Schmitz), 16 wooden
table (© MaxPhotographer), 17 (© Jostein Hauge), 18
witch (© Fer Gregory), 18 toad (© alexsvirid), 19 toad (©
Angelo Giampiccolo), 19 male hand (© hans.slegers),
20 cow (© arniep), 20 map (© Atlaspix), 20 weather
symbols (© mesimply), 22 lemon shark (© FAUP), 22
hypnotic whirlpool eye (© Biczó Zsolt), 22 silver pocket
watch (© Graça Victoria), 22 water background (©
Clover), 24 (© Daniel Alvarez), 25 (© Bridgena Barnard),
26 (© Matej Kastelic), 27 red sports car (© Charlie
Hutton), 27 skittles (© Becky Stares), 27 bull (© Vera
Zinkova), 27 coloured footballs (© Perry Correll), 28
goldfish (© dibrova), 28 gameshow host (© criben), 29
(© Richard Peterson).

Cover photographs of walrus (© Nejron Photo) and
saxophone (© kuznetcov_konstantin) reproduced with
permission of Shutterstock.

We would like to thank Diana Bentley and Marla Conn
for their invaluable help in the preparation of this book.

CONTENTS

Some words are shown in bold, **like this**. You can find out what they mean by looking in the glossary.

COULD A WALRUS PLAY THE SAXOPHONE?

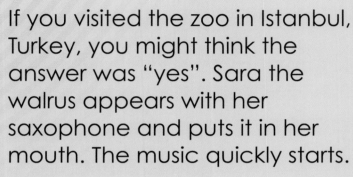

If you visited the zoo in Istanbul, Turkey, you might think the answer was "yes". Sara the walrus appears with her saxophone and puts it in her mouth. The music quickly starts.

Sadly, walruses aren't equipped to play the saxophone in real life. Sara is just **miming**. The music actually comes from a sound system!

Big flippers + tiny buttons = impossible to play notes!

WHAT ARE CROCODILE TEARS?

Crocodiles do not cry because they are sad! The crying actually happens when they eat. This is because crocodiles cannot chew. They have to swallow their food in big chunks. Gulping down these chunks forces **fluid** from **glands** around their eyes.

BOO HOO!

A crocodile's tears are difficult to spot because they are always soaking wet!

COULD AN EARWIG CRAWL INTO YOUR EAR?

Even medical books used to say that earwigs sometimes crawled into people's ears. Earwigs *do* like warm, moist places. Fortunately, though, these places do *not* include human ears!

Did you know?
Although earwigs have wings, they hardly ever fly.

Earwigs were named because of the shape of their wings. When stretched out, they look like human ears.

CAN YOU CURE A JELLYFISH STING BY WEEING ON IT?

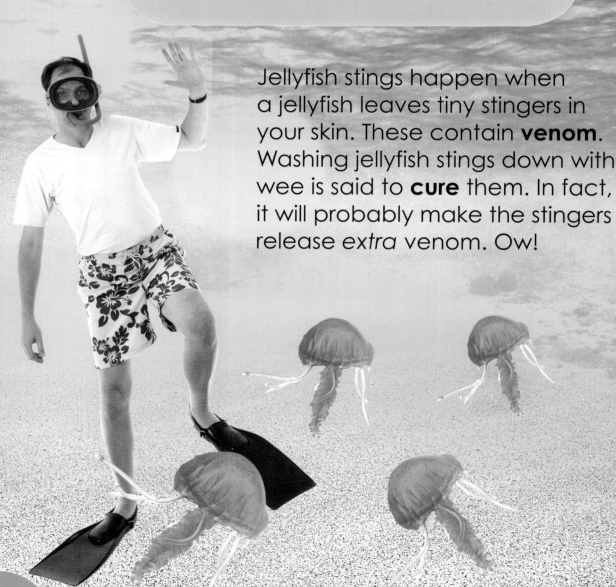

Jellyfish stings happen when a jellyfish leaves tiny stingers in your skin. These contain **venom**. Washing jellyfish stings down with wee is said to **cure** them. In fact, it will probably make the stingers release *extra* venom. Ow!

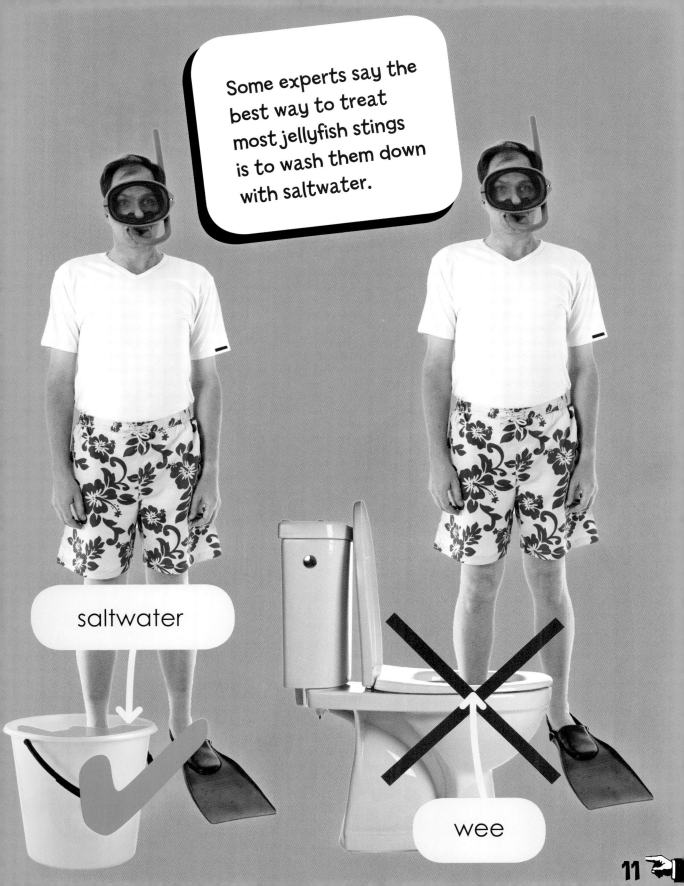

11

COULD COWS REALLY DESTROY THE WORLD?

Have cows perhaps developed a super bomb to blow us all up? No! It's cow farts people worry about. Cow farts are said to contain gases that cause **global warming** to get worse.

mOOOO!

This is wrong, of course. It's cow burps, not farts, which could destroy the world!

cow fart does little harm

cow burp contains gas that is terrible for the environment

DOES CUTTING A WORM IN HALF MAKE TWO WORMS?

No. If you accidentally cut a garden worm in two, the best result would be:

- one shorter worm
- one dead bit of worm.

A worm can only survive being cut in two if it happens near its tail. If you cut it in the middle, both parts would wriggle as if they were alive. Then they would die.

15

DO DOGS LEAVE FINGERPRINTS?

No – but if you think Fido's been stealing your biscuits, there might be another way to find out. Each dog's nose print is as **unique** as a human fingerprint.

"It wasn't me... honest!"

tiny lines

shape of nostrils

Did you know?
Up to a third of a dog's brain may be used for smells!

CAN YOU CATCH WARTS FROM A TOAD?

Toads do *look* warty. It's no wonder people used to think they could catch **warts** from them. In fact, the lumps and bumps on a toad's skin aren't warts at all. They are **glands**. When a toad is scared, the glands release a slimy liquid called mucus. Some toads can even release poison!

CAN COWS FORECAST THE WEATHER?

It's claimed that cows lie down when they sense rain is on its way. This is not true, though. Cows actually lie down after eating food.

And now for the weather ...

Did you know?

Some animals do seem to be able to **predict** storms:

- Sharks head for deep water
- Birds go to their nests
- Bees shelter in their **hives**

CAN YOU HYPNOTIZE A SHARK?

Sharks are feared around the world. But some sharks can be **hypnotized** – just by rubbing the tip of their nose! Even deadly killers such as the great white shark can be affected.

How to hypnotize a shark

Step 1. Rub shark's nose
Step 2. Stand shark on head
Step 3. Rub nose more

Shark is hypnotized
for 15 minutes!

Did you know?
In 1997, a killer whale
was seen hypnotizing
a great white shark –
which it then ate!

DO HYENAS REALLY LAUGH?

Hyenas crunch through bone with their powerful jaws. They can run faster than a man. They're so nasty, people even say hyenas laugh when they kill something. This is not actually true, though. The noise *sounds* like laughter to us. But it's just one hyena telling another that it can eat first.

Ha! Ha!

DOES RED REALLY MAKE BULLS ANGRY?

There's an old saying that something that makes you angry is, "like a red rag to a bull". In fact, bulls may not even see red. They are quite likely to confuse it with blue or green.

Is it the red **cape** making this bull angry – or the man sticking hooks in him?

Actually, they all look green to me. Or is it blue?

DO GOLDFISH REALLY HAVE BAD MEMORIES?

Goldfish are said to have 3-second memories. In fact, they are quite good at remembering things. Goldfish have been taught to fetch objects and other tricks. They even remember the tricks months later.

What is the capital of France?

Umm...

GLOSSARY

cape sleeveless coat that does up around the neck and hangs down around your body

cure make someone who is unwell better

fluid liquid without a fixed shape, such as water

gland part of an animal that releases liquid

global warming increase in Earth's temperature. Global warming is responsible for changes in our weather and more natural disasters.

hive place where bees live

hypnotize put into a dreamy state of mind, in which you do not act for yourself

miming pretending you are doing something, but without actually doing it

predict say what will happen in the future

unique one of a kind

venom substance that is harmful when injected under the skin

wart small, hard lump on the skin

FIND OUT MORE

Books

Animal Top Tens series, Anita Ganeri (Raintree, 2009)

Animals: A Children's Encyclopedia (Dorling Kindersley, 2008)

Wild Animal Atlas (National Geographic Kids, 2010)

You Swallow Spiders In Your Sleep! The Fact or Fiction Behind Animals (Truth or Busted), Paul Mason (Wayland, 2012)

Websites

www.kidsbiology.com/animals-for-children.php
There are hundreds of different animals to discover on this website.

kids.nationalgeographic.com/kids/animals/ creaturefeature
This website allows you to find out more about your favourite animals.

INDEX